How to Play the Piano
Chords Method

level
1

D1613072

Ages 8+
(or with a teacher)

About Fingerprint Music

Fingerprint Music is a company that specializes in the publication of educational materials for piano and guitar. Founded in 2006 by Jacob Black, the company started out as a music school in Kansas City. In 2013, Fingerprint Music expanded to Seattle and continued to grow its reputation as a trusted source for high-quality music education. In 2021, the company started a publishing division to share its expertise with a wider audience. Going forward, Fingerprint Music plans to offer a range of books, videos, and audio resources for aspiring musicians.

Contents

i. How to Find Your Musical Fingerprint

The Fingerprint Method encourages you to find your own unique musical path. The approach to playing the piano in this book— using **Chords**— is one possible musical path for the piano, but not the only one. If you don't feel this path speaks to you, you may wish to try out a different one— the paths in the Fingerprint method also include learning how to **Play By Ear, Improvise, Write Songs**, or **Read Sheet Music**. With the right instruction, even total beginners can start with any of these approaches. Or, you might want to try learning from videos instead of books. You might even want to try out a different instrument. (Fingerprint plans to offer a range of books, videos, and audio resources for all of the above.)

Everyone is unique. We encourage you to experiment with different musical paths, because each path will only be a good fit for *some* people— but every human is musical. Music is like language— everyone is wired for it, but in different ways. The question isn't "am I musical?" but "*how* am I musical?" The answer is what we call your **musical fingerprint.**

When you find the right musical path for you, it should feel natural and fun. So if this book doesn't feel that way for you, we bet a different approach will.

Each of our series will have a **beginner crash course** in book one of the series that enables you to jump right in with no prior knowledge (or you can skip it if you know the basics). Each one of our series will stand alone and will get you up and running playing music and having fun.

If you're playing music as a hobby, you'll have lots of fun learning a few things to help you sound good fast while squeezing music into your busy life. (Even if you only play occasionally and progress is slow, playing music is more than worthwhile for its emotionally expressive, meditative, & brain-exercising benefits.)

And if you're a serious student of music, each of these approaches is one piece of the larger puzzle of overall musical fluency. If you study all of them, and you learn to **play chords**, **play by ear**, **improvise**, **write songs**, *and* **read music**, you'll become a very versatile and skilled musician.

Just like language, learning music *can* be a very natural, human process. All you have to do is follow your own interests and strengths and find the way of being musical that feels the most like YOU. That, and don't give up!

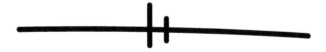

ii. A Note On (Not) Reading Music

There's a common myth about playing the piano— that you have to read music to do it. Well, it's time to debunk that myth.

Reading music is a great skill to have if you want to learn complicated music with a high level of technical precision. It's also a time-saving and space-saving way to communicate musical ideas once you get it down.

BUT it's by no means the only way to learn the piano (or any other instrument). And for many people, focusing on reading music from the start just takes all the fun out of it! It turns what could be an joyous musical adventure in creating colorful sounds into a draining technical exercise.

Think of music as a language. As small children, we learn language by speaking it first; reading and writing comes later. Imagine how hard it would be for kids if we made them learn to read before speaking.

Of course, for some people, reading music from the start *does* work well— their brains have a knack for the logic of it. (Just like some kids may show more comfort with reading than speaking.) But for many others, learning to "speak" music before reading it makes more sense.

So, if reading music isn't the only way to learn, what other ways are there?

6

This book offers one possible answer: learning to play using **chords** and **chord progressions**. There are other ways, too, covered in other planned Fingerprint series, such as: learning to **play by ear**, how to **improvise** using scales, or **songwriting**, none of which requires reading music.

The Fingerprint Method is not against reading music— we're just pro-FUN, and what's fun very much depends on you. And like we said, reading music does work well for some people. So we also have a planned series with our unique approach to learning to **Read Music**, which you can delve into (or not) at any point in your musical development.

If you think learning to play from chords could be the right musical path for you, or if you're not sure what it means to play from chords and you want to find out… then let's get started.

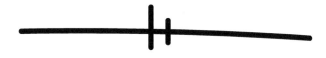

iii. What You Can Do with Chords

Before we zoom in and put your fingers on the keys, let's zoom out for a second and talk about where this path leads.

Once you get playing with chords down (which you'll do by the end of this series), you'll be able to play *lots* of songs *very* quickly. Using chords, you can sit down and play a chord version of almost any song with little or no rehearsal. Chords are a set of tools you learn once— and then use to play almost any song you want.

Of course, you don't have to learn *lots* of songs— maybe you'll want to focus on going deeper with a smaller number of songs. Either way, you'll have a complete set of tools to play a chord version of any song of your choosing.

Pretty much any song can be simplified and broken apart into a **melody** (the part you'd sing or hum) and a series of chords that go with the melody, known as the **chord progression** or the **harmony**.

The **chord progression** for almost any published song is easy to find online— just search for "[Name of Song] [Name of Artist] **Chords**" and the first result is often exactly what you're looking for. For example, you could type this into the search bar:

```
Bridge Over Troubled Water Simon & Garfunkel Chords
```

The website *UltimateGuitar.com*, despite the name, works well for our purposes on the piano and is often at the top as of 2022. (More details on how to learn a song from the internet are in Chapter 9.)

Playing a song from its chord progression can work especially well if you want to **sing the melody** along with your piano playing. Or if you want to **accompany someone else** while they sing the melody or play it on another instrument. Or if you just want to **leave the melody out**. Playing *just* the chord progression of a song, especially with a little style, often sounds great even without the melody.

Playing *just* the chord progression without the melody is called playing the **accompaniment**. Or in jazz lingo, **comping**. (This book is essentially Comping 101.)

Learning the chord progression of a song is also a great way to quickly understand its underlying structure. When you learn the chord progression of a song, you can recreate the song in your own way without playing the exact instrument parts from the original recording (or the original sheet music).

On one hand, this means you can quickly play a very simple piano part for any song by following its chord progression. This is great for impromptu singalongs or jam sessions, or if you just want to dabble with a song without intending to master it.

On the other hand, you can use the chord progression as a jumping-off point to learn the song in great detail, or even to craft your own alternative "cover" version.

Learning to play songs from their chords is also a great step toward writing your own songs. (To take the next step and understand how to fit chords together to write a song, watch for our planned series on **Songwriting**.)

Alternatives to Playing from Chords

The Fingerprint Method is all about options— so if leaving out the melody and focusing on playing just the accompaniment seems highly unnatural to you, that may be a sign that you would prefer learning to **Play By Ear**, where typically the focus would be on melody first, adding accompaniment later.

Or, if you prefer to learn the actual version from the original recording or the original sheet music, or if you want to play the melody & accompaniment *together* from the start, you may be interested in learning to **Read Music** on the piano, or **Read Tab** on the guitar.

If any book or series doesn't *click* with you after awhile, that may be a sign that a different path would work better. There are many ways to unlock the musical universe.

If you're still on board with chords, continue on…

Beginner's Crash Course

(if you know the names of all the notes on the piano, you may skip to page 33, but may also find starting at page 24 interesting)

The first thing to notice when you look at the keyboard is the white keys and black keys, and how the black keys are organized— into **groups of 2** and **groups of 3**. These groups are the landmarks that help you find your way around the keyboard.

On a full-sized 88-key keyboard like this one, there's also one black key by itself at the far left:

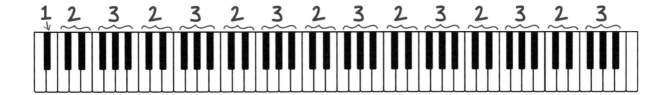

But smaller keyboards (often 61 keys, like this one) usually start with a group of two at the far left:

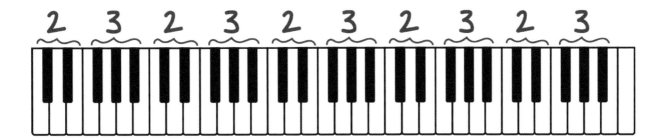

Naming White Notes

Each white note is named with a letter from the **musical alphabet**. The musical alphabet has only seven letters: **A B C D E F G**

When you get to **G**, you just start over again with **A**. On a full-sized keyboard, with the one lone black key at the left, just start at **A** and go through the musical alphabet over and over:

If your keyboard starts with a group of two black keys at the far left, start on **C** the first time, then start over with **A**:

Each letter is used many times on the piano. And every time it's used, the white key it falls on looks the same. For example, every **E** on the piano looks the same— it's just to the right of a group of two black notes. All the **E**'s look like this:

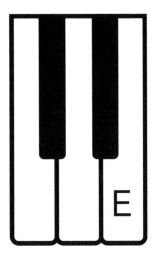

Or to put it another way, like this:

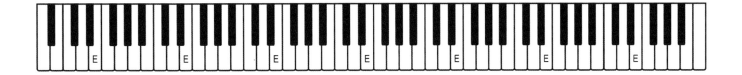

13

Each letter of the musical alphabet looks the same every time it occurs on the keyboard. Here are all 7:

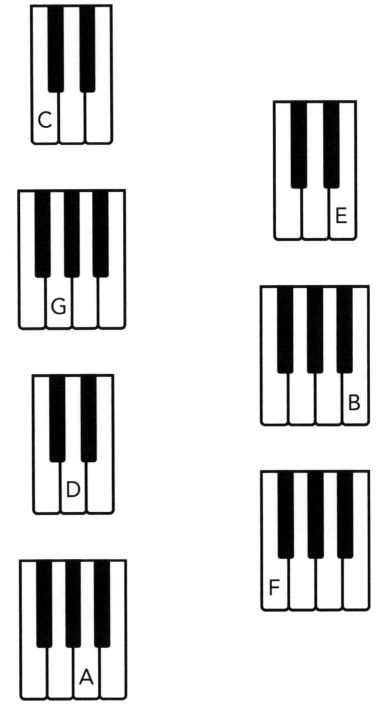

The best way to learn these is to go through and play all the notes on the piano for each letter, from lowest to highest and back again.

Let's start with all of the **F**'s.

Play them from left to right and back again:

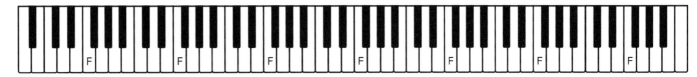

(If you have a pedal, try holding it down while you do this. Sounds pretty cool. If you have three pedals, use the one on the right.)

Next, all of the **C**'s:

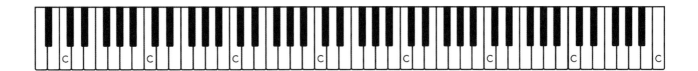

Notice that the highest **C**, furthest to the right, looks different than the others, because the keyboard ends right before there would be another group of 2 black keys. So there's no black key to cut a piece out of the **C**, making it the only rectangular white key on the keyboard.

We can also determine that the highest note is **C** by noticing that other **C**'s are also 2 white keys above (to the right of) the nearest group of 3:

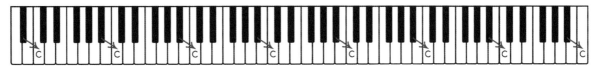

Now, let's play all of the **G**'s:

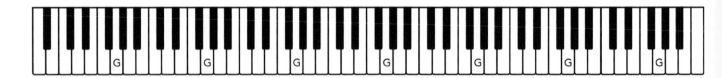

then the **D**'s:

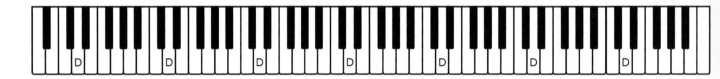

and the **A**'s:

On a full-sized (88-key) keyboard, the lowest **A** doesn't look like the other **A**'s, similar the highest **C** described above. Like we noticed before, at the very lowest (left) end of the keyboard, there's just one black key where there would be three. That one black key *would be* part of a group of 3 if the keyboard didn't stop there, so **A** is to its left.

We can also determine this by noting that every **A** is 2 white keys below **C**:

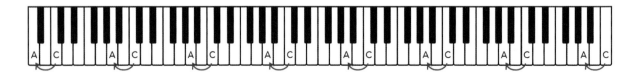

Now the **E**'s:

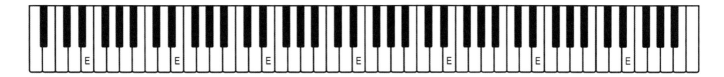

Lastly, the **B**'s:

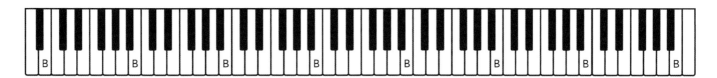

You may be wondering why we took you through them in a strange order: **F, C, G, D, A, E, B.** This order follows something called the *Circle of Fifths*, which means it will sound nice and musical to play the notes in this order. Learning this order will also be helpful if you go on to learn about the Circle of Fifths in music theory.

Practicing the notes "out of order" like this also helps you memorize each one independently instead of only thinking of them in sequence. But— we recommend that you also practice them in sequence to maximize your familiarity.

To practice in sequence, play the notes from left to right while naming them out loud.

This is easy going up, or to the right. Find a low **A** to start on, and then play the keys from left to right as you say the musical alphabet out loud (or at least "out loud" in your head). When you get to **G**, start over with **A**. Don't feel like you need to do the entire keyboard— 3 times through the alphabet is enough:

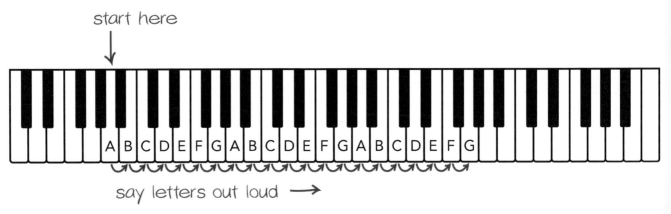

The harder part is going backwards. This time play the notes from right to left starting from **G** and going backwards in the musical alphabet, like this:

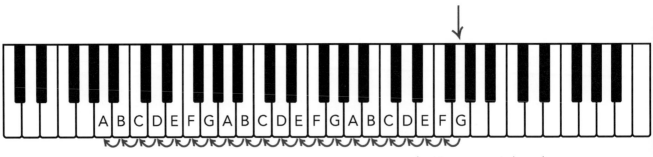

Try to do this without looking at this page if you can. One easy way to get better at this is just to say the backwards sequence over and over until you memorize it:

"G F E D C B A… G F E D C B A… G F E D C B A…"

Naming Black Notes

Every black note has **two names**. (There's a reason for this in music theory, but for now, we're just gonna teach you what the two names are.)

To name black notes, we start with the same seven letters of the musical alphabet: **A**, **B**, **C**, **D**, **E**, **F**, & **G**, but then we add a symbol afterwards— either ♯ (pronounced "sharp") or ♭ (pronounced "flat").

Sharp (♯) means up. Which on the piano, means *to the right*.

So this black note—

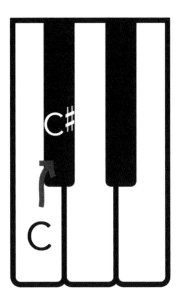

—since it's one *to the right* of **C**, or one *up* from **C**, is called **C**♯ (**pronounced "C sharp"**).

Likewise, this note—

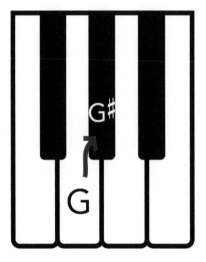

—is one to the right of **G**, so we call it **G**♯ ("G sharp").

Now, we can name **all of the black notes using their sharp names:**

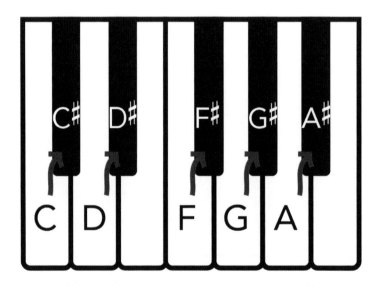

Like we said, each black note has *two* names. The other one is "Flat" (♭).

Flat (♭) means down. On the piano, *down* means *to the left.*

So this note—

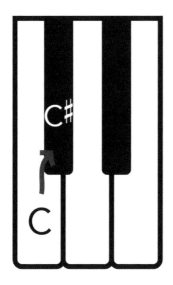 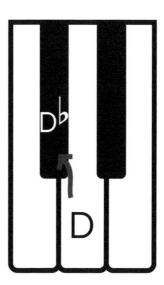

—can be called **C♯** ("C Sharp"), as we saw, or it can be called **D♭** ("D flat"), since it's *one to the left* of **D**; in other words, it's one *down* from **D**.

21

Likewise, this note can be called **F♯** ("F Sharp") or **G♭** ("G Flat"):

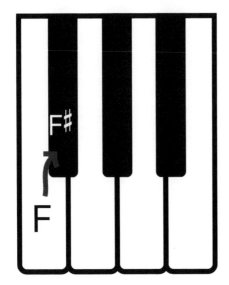
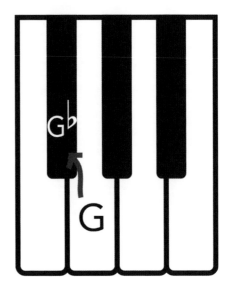

Now, we can name **all of the black notes using their flat names:**

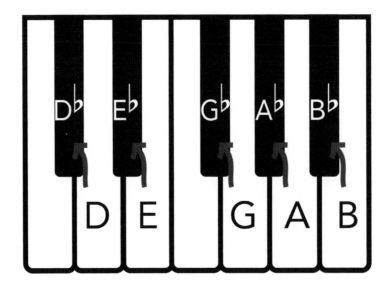

Putting it all together, each black note has two options:

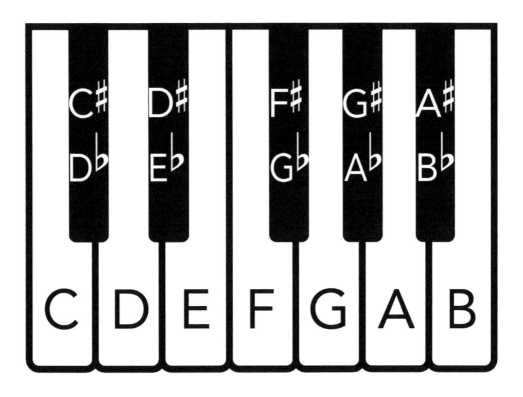

Visit fingerprintmusic.co/pianochords1 for a
printable PDF of this page and other key
reference pages from this book.

Congrats— you can now name all the notes! Continue on to learn a different system that many countries in the world use to name notes (p. 24-26), as well as some rare exceptions where we use different names for notes (p. 27-32). Or, feel free to skip one or both parts and get started learning chords (p. 33) right now.

Optional Section: Naming Notes using "Fixed Do"

(Skip to page 33 to get started playing chords.)

There's also an entirely different system of note-naming that's widely used across the world, including in Spain, Portugal, France, Italy, Belgium, Romania, Latin American countries, French-speaking Canada, Bosnia and Herzegovina, Croatia, Russia, Serbia, Poland, Ukraine, Georgia, Bulgaria, Greece, Armenia, Albania, North Macedonia, Mongolia, Iran, Israel, the Arab world, Turkey, and Taiwan.

Instead of "**C**, **D**, **E**, **F**, **G**, **A**, & **B**" for the white keys, this system uses "**Do**, **Re**, **Mi**, **Fa**, **Sol**, **La**, & **Si** *[not Ti]*." (Pronounced "doe, ray, me, fah, sole, lah, see.") **Do** is "fixed" on C, so we call this system **Fixed Do.**

So, instead of this:

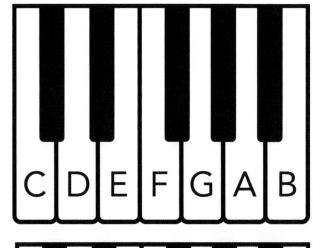

Fixed Do uses this:

FYI— there's another system that sounds very similar, called **Moveable Do,** that's used to teach singing and ear training. **Moveable Do** is famously referenced in "Doe, A Deer" from *The Sound of Music*. In **Moveable Do**, **Do** isn't "fixed" on C— **Do** moves to whichever note is the root note, or "home" note, of the song. Also, the syllables used are usually slightly different than **Fixed Do:** "**Do**, **Re**, **Mi**, **Fa**, **So** *[instead of Sol]*, **La**, & **Ti** *[instead of Si]*." More about **Movable Do** will be in our planned series on how to **Play By Ear.**

For black notes in **Fixed Do**, we still use the same modifier symbols, but we say different words for them:

♯ **is pronounced "dièse"** ("dee-**Ehz**," from French) instead of "sharp," and

♭ **is pronounced "bemolle"** ("bay-**Mol**-leh," from Italian) instead of "flat."

So this note is either **Do**♯ ("Do dièse") or **Re**♭ ("Re bemolle"):

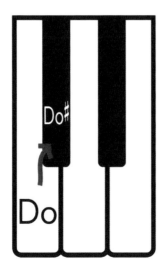
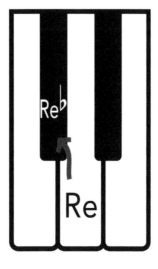

Putting it all together with Fixed Do note names:

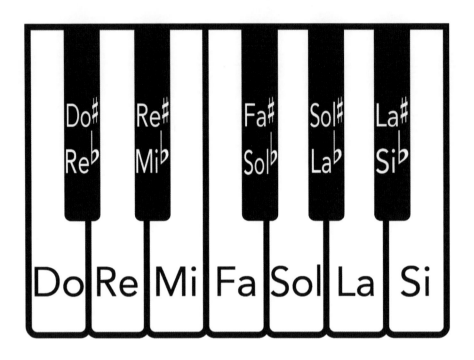

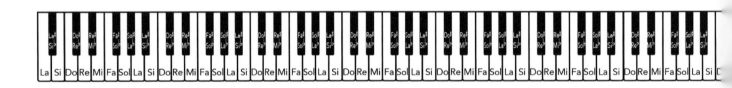

For the rest of the book, we'll return to using the **musical alphabet** to name notes, not **Fixed Do**. Refer back to this section if you need to "translate" anything to or from Fixed Do.

Optional Section: Rare Note Names

(Skip to page 33 to get started playing chords.)

You'll rarely come across the note names in this section, if at all, but you might want to know about them just in case.

First of all, you might come across one of these notes: **B**♯, **C**♭, **E**♯, or **F**♭. These are special cases because they're sharps and flats that are *white keys* on the piano, not black.

Let's start with **B**♯ ("B Sharp")— since # means *one to the right,* this is **B**♯:

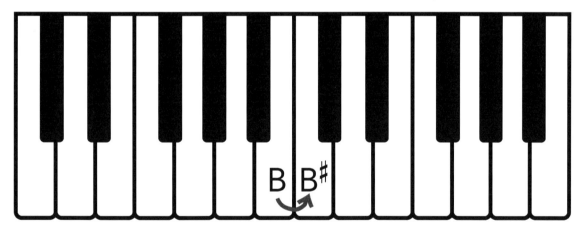

The usual name for this note is, of course, just **C**. But once in awhile, you may see it written as **B**♯. (For music theory reasons beyond this book.)

Same thing With **C♭** ("C Flat"), usually just called **B**:

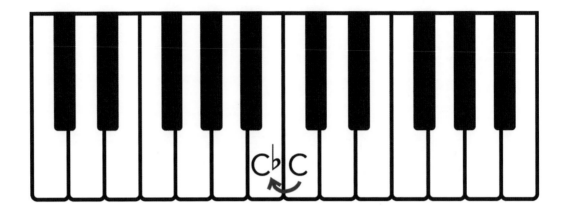

E♯ ("E Sharp") is usually known as **F**:

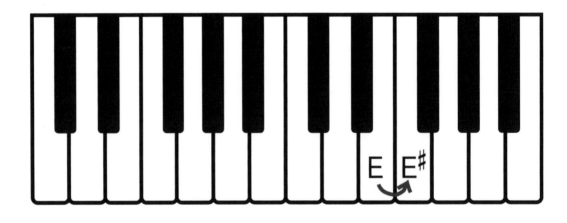

And **F♭** ("F Flat") is usually known as **E**:

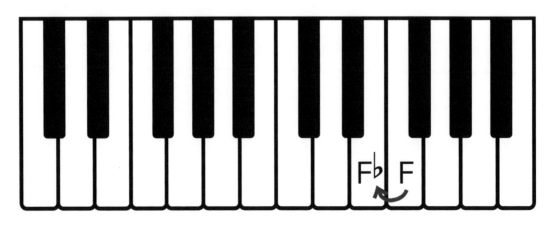

28

To get even weirder, sometimes notes are named using **"double sharp" (✖)** or **"double flat" (♭♭)**. This just means that you go *up two notes (for* ✖*)* or *down two notes (for* ♭♭*)*.

So this note is **F✖** ("F double sharp"), usually known as **G**:

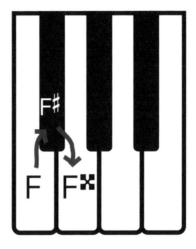

This is **E✖** ("E double sharp"), usually known as **F♯** ("F sharp") or **G♭** ("G flat"):

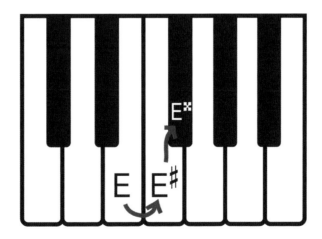

This note is **E𝄫** ("E double flat"), commonly known as **D**:

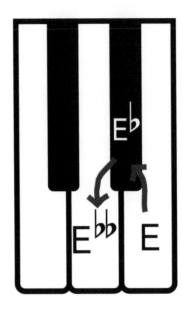

This is **C𝄫** ("C double flat"), commonly known as **B♭** ("B flat") or **A♯** ("A sharp"):

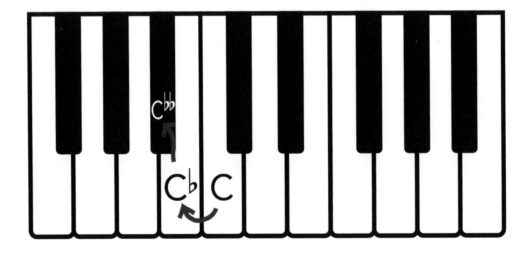

30

This results in an explosion of possibilities. Now, most notes, white and black, have *three* possible names, except for the middle of the three black notes, which just has two:

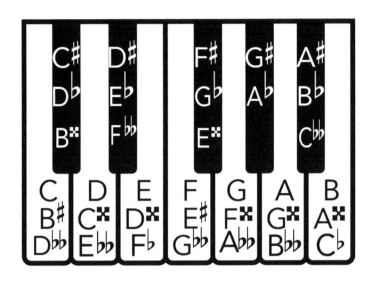

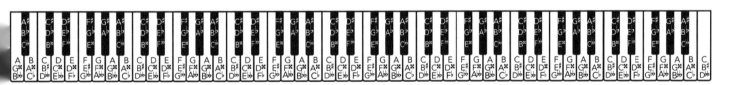

Yikes. But don't worry— you probably won't ever see this. It's mostly just fun to geek out with all these diagrams. Double sharps and double flats are pretty rare in chord charts.

Most of the time, you'll use ♯ (Sharp) and ♭ (Flat) to refer *only* to black notes, and you won't have to worry about double sharps or double flats or double trouble of any kind!

31

Lastly, one other symbol you may come across:

♮ (pronounced "Natural")

This is used to *cancel* a sharp or flat.

There are times when reading music that you would assume a note is sharp or flat *unless* a natural sign cancels it out. You'll rarely if ever encounter this when playing chords, but now you know— natural just means it's *not* sharp or flat. In other words:

A ♮ ("A Natural") just means **A.**

B ♮ ("B Natural") just means **B.**

C ♮ ("C Natural") just means **C.**

Etc.

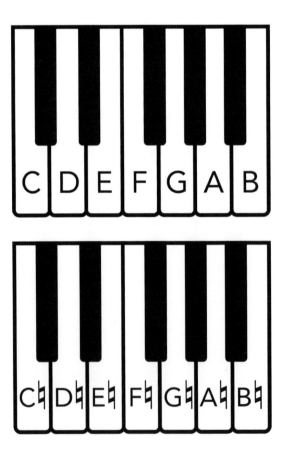

1. Intro to Major and Minor Chords

You can play a ton of songs using only **Major** and **Minor chords**, so we're going to start with those two before branching out to other types of chords. (suspended, diminished, augmented, extended chords, and more are covered in later books.)

To Western-conditioned ears,* it's often said that **major chords sound *happy*** and **minor chords sound *sad*.**

Rather than happy and sad, we think it's more accurate to say **major is *light*** and **minor is *dark*.** How a chord "feels" depends in part on what comes before and after it in a song, just like how a color feels in a painting depends on what's around it. A minor chord can add sweetness to a major-key song, and a major chord can sound like a dark descent in a minor key. But listening to each chord by itself, you can hear a contrast in feel between the lighter major and the darker minor.

Hearing major as happy and minor as sad seems to be culturally conditioned at least in part— the major/minor dichotomy of Western tonality is irrelevant or sometimes flipped in many other musical traditions, including Arabic maqam, Indian ragas, Javanese slendro, and others.

Let's learn how to play some chords.

We're going to start with your **right hand only**.

We'll play a bunch of chords using **only fingers 1, 3, and 5** in the right hand.

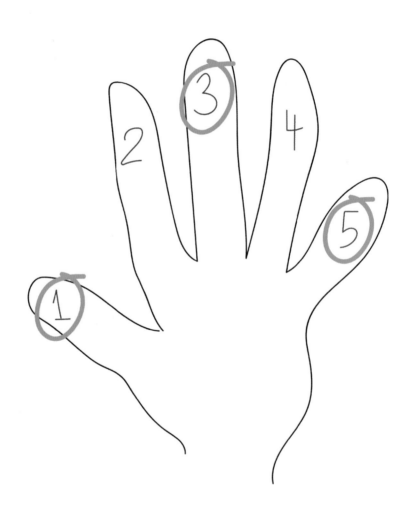

Here's a chord diagram for a **C Major** chord:

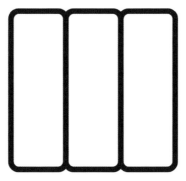

Note that this is a special kind of diagram the Fingerprint Method uses; if you mention this to other piano players they may not know what you're talking about.

This means there are 3 white notes in this chord (which we'll play with fingers 1, 3, and 5).

Start by putting **finger 1** (your thumb) of your **right hand** on the note that matches the name of the chord, known as its **root note**. For **C Major**, the **root note** is **C**. **Find a C near the middle of the keyboard** and place **finger 1 (your thumb)** on it. Don't play it yet, just rest your thumb on it for now while we place the other fingers:

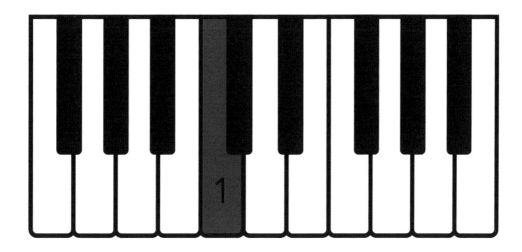

Then you can add the other two white notes with fingers 3 & 5:

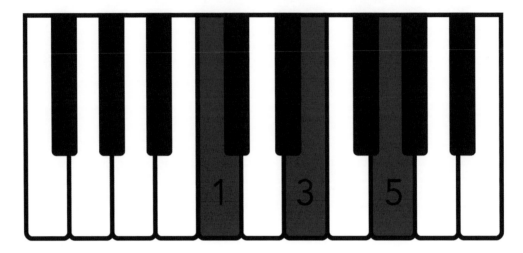

Play the chord by pressing all three notes down at the same time. (It can take some practice to hold up fingers 2 and 4 enough that you don't press down the notes in between.)

Notice how far apart your fingers are— a comfortable, relaxed distance, and with skipped notes in between. **Your fingers will be about the same distance apart for all the other major chords.** Knowing this, you can figure out how to play a chord using just a diagram like this, showing that this chord is all white notes:

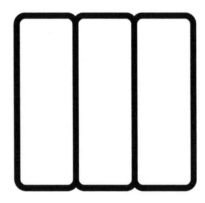

We like using these color-block diagrams instead of showing you exactly which notes to play, because it helps you focus on the **chord shape** and what it *looks like* on the piano. Most of the time, your fingers will naturally find the right notes if you know the shape and don't stretch or squish them. You can also use your ear to help you figure out if you're playing the chord right— if it sounds strange when you play it, you may have a wrong note.

Now let's look at the chord diagram for **C Minor**:

Again, start by putting **finger 1** (your thumb) of your **right hand** on the root note of the chord. For **C Minor**, the root note is **C. Find a C near the middle of the keyboard.** Don't play it yet, just rest your thumb on it for now:

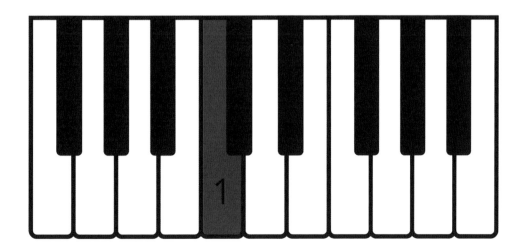

As the chord diagram shows, the outside notes are white, with a black note in the middle:

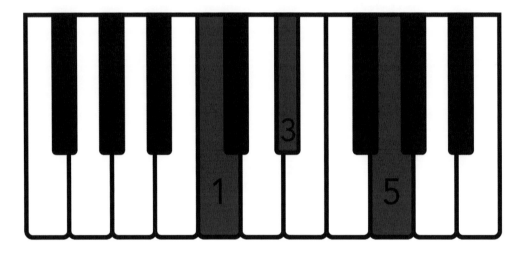

Use fingers 1, 3, and 5, and **play the chord** by pressing all three notes down at the same time.

Again, notice the shape of your hand. The middle finger has to reach a little to the left compared with the major shape. **All of the minor chords we learn will have about this same distance between notes.**

Congrats! You've played your first major and minor chords. Now, let's add a left hand note to make them sound richer and deeper.

2. Adding A Left Hand Note

Your left hand's job is easy for now— it plays one single note while your right hand plays the chord. The note your left hand plays is the **root note** of the chord, or its namesake.

So while your right hand plays a chord (in this case, **C Minor** again), your left hand uses **any finger** to play a low **root note** (in this case, **C**):

And here's the same thing for **C Major**:

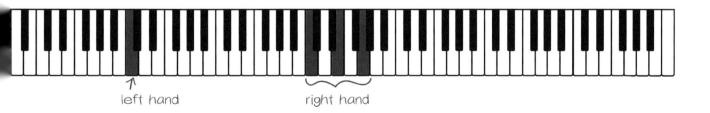

You can place the right hand and left hand in any **octave**, which just means higher or lower versions of the same notes. Most will sound good, and it's fun to hear the wide array of colorful options.

Here are a few other ways to play **C Minor** using various octaves in your left and right hands:

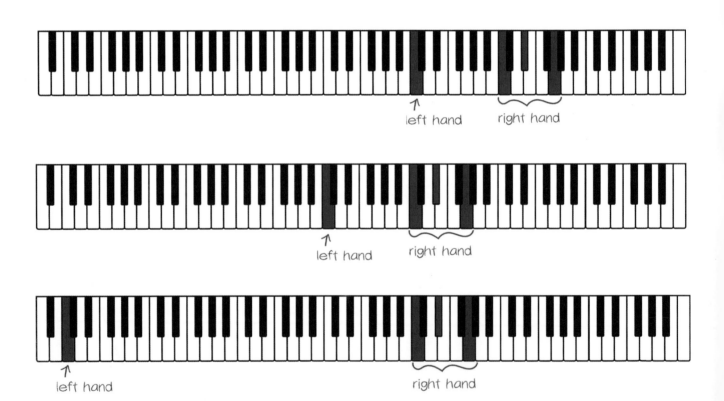

Try other combinations on your own. You may notice that once you pass a certain point, playing a chord too low (too far to the left) doesn't sound clear anymore.

3. Chords That Start On White Notes

Okay, so we've learned one major chord and one minor chord. There are **12 Major Chords** and **12 Minor Chords** in all.

We're going to start by learning 7 of each— the ones with white notes as root notes, since these are a little easier. (There are 7 white notes, and each one has a Major and a Minor chord.)

We'll learn the other 5 Majors and 5 Minors (the ones with black notes as root notes) in chapter 6.

Here are **all the major and minor chords that start on white notes:**

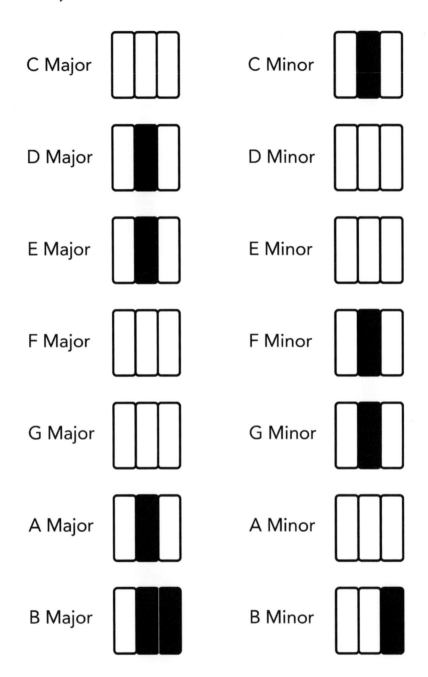

Try playing these in order— first all the majors in the left column from top to bottom, then all the minors on the right. Try them with or without a left hand root note. Try to play them using these chord diagrams alone. Remember, your fingers will always be about the same distance apart as they were for C Major and C Minor. But if you get stuck (say, on **B Major** or others), **use pages 82-85 to get unstuck.**

Here are the **same chords** from the last page, but in a different order that will help your brain make a connection between similar chords:

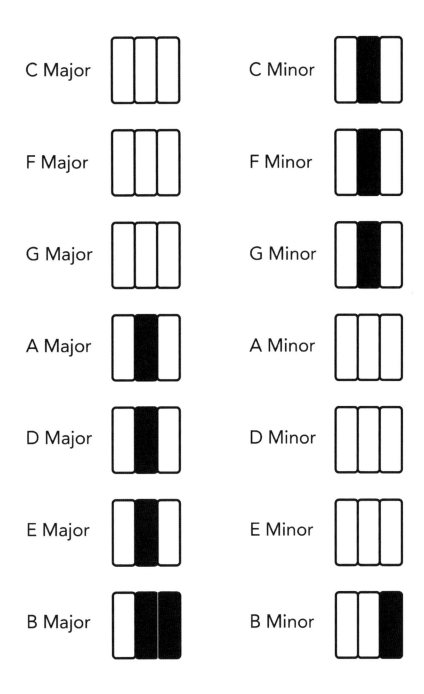

Again, play the majors first and then the minors. Try with and without a left-hand root note. **Try practicing them in both orders (from this page and the previous one)** to maximize your familiarity. Again, refer to pages 82-85 if you get stuck.

4. Intro to Playing Chord Progressions

Okay, let's try making some real music now.
Here's a *very** common chord progression:

C   G   Am   F

These are **chord symbols**, an abbreviated way to write the names of chords. In chord symbol lingo, a **lowercase "m" means Minor**, and *nothing* **means Major.** So we can translate these chord symbols:

C = C Major
G = G Major
Am = A minor
F = F Major

Let's review the chord diagrams for these four:

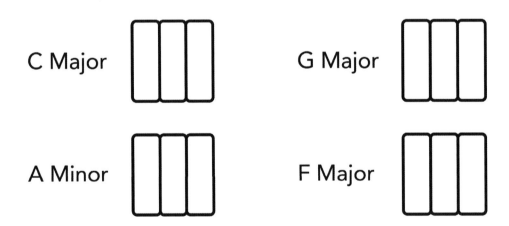

*These four chords (in various keys) are used in many, many, *many* songs. Search YouTube for "Axis of Awesome - Four Chord Song" to see what we mean.

Here's the first chord, **C Major**, with right and left hand:

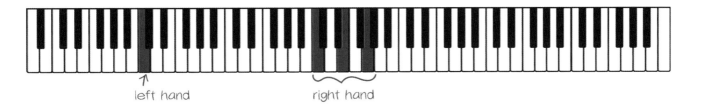

We're going to give all of these chords **4** counts— the most common rhythm. In other songs, chords may also get **2** or **3** counts, or multiples of these like **6** or **8** counts. We'll cover rhythm in a more precise way later, but many people find they can "fake it" and figure out by listening how many counts to give each chord in a song.

To get a rhythm going, hold the left-hand note while your right hand plays the chord **4** times with a steady beat:

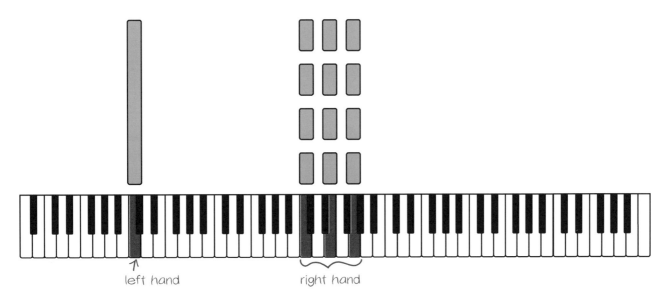

(If you have a pedal, try holding it down while you do this. Sounds cool with or without. If you have a piano with three pedals, or two, use the one on the right.)

Or you could hold down the right-hand chord while playing the left-hand note **4** times:

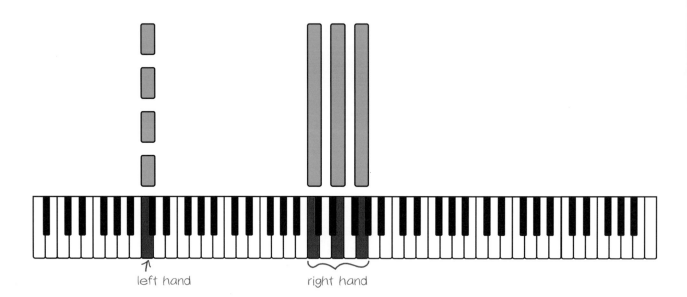

left hand

right hand

Each of these gives a distinctly different feel. You might consider playing the first one slower, and the second one faster. Use whichever one you like, or invent your own.

Here's the second chord, **G Major**:

left hand   right hand

Try it the same way, holding your left or right hand while the other plays **4** counts:

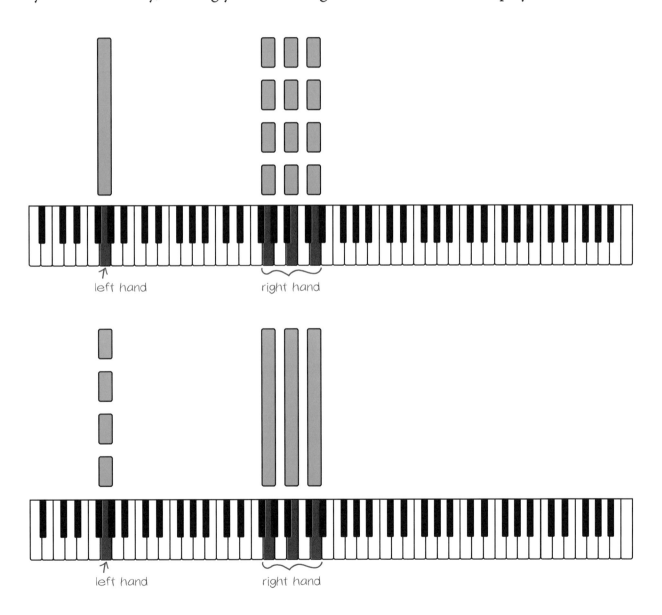

left hand   right hand

left hand   right hand

Now, try playing **4 counts on C** and then **4 counts on G**. Go back and forth a few times. (If you use the pedal while doing this, lift the pedal up and press it down again to *reset* the sound when you switch to a new chord.)

When you're comfortable moving between **C** and **G**, here's **A Minor**:

Try it the same way, playing four counts with either your right or left hand. When you're ready, play the whole thing so far: **4 counts on C, 4 counts on G**, and **4 counts on Am**.

And then the last chord, **F Major**:

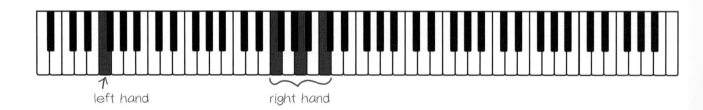

Now you can play the whole chord progression, with **4** counts each:

C   G   Am   F

Like many songs do, you can just repeat this chord progression on a **loop**:

C G Am F / C G Am F / C G Am F etc.

End on whichever chord you like. Ending on **C** will sound the most resolved, followed by **Am**, then **G**, and **F** will sound the least resolved.

Congratulations! You can now play the chords for approximately 27 million songs… and we're just gettin' warmed up. As soon as you learn chords with black note roots, you'll be ready to learn all your favorites.

Broken Chords

Now let's add a little variety to the right hand.

Instead of playing all 3 notes in the chord at the same time, you can split them up. We call this using a **Broken Chord,** or **Arpeggio.**

You can play the notes from the chord in any combination or order you like. Let's try a couple of common examples.

First, try playing the chord one note at a time in a back and forth pattern, like this:

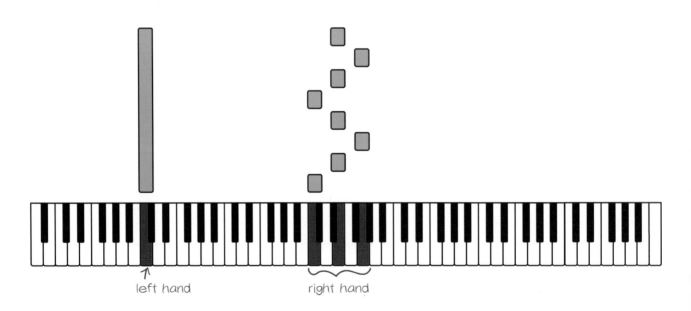

(One example of a song based on this pattern is *Someone Like You* by Adele.)

Then, try playing the top two notes followed by the low note, like this:

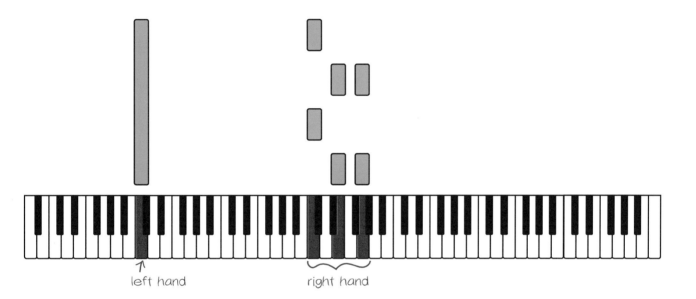

left hand   right hand

(One example of a song based on this pattern is *Let it Be* by the Beatles.)

Or, invent patterns of your own!

Now let's try that same 4-chord progression, but in a different key. That means we'll use completely different chords, but they'll have the same basic sound and feel because they relate to each other in the same way.

So here's another version of the infamous 4-chord progression:

G   D   Em   C

As a reminder,

G = G Major
D = D Major
Em = E Minor
C = C Major

Let's review the chord diagrams for these four:

G Major

D Major

E Minor

C Major

Here's the first chord, **G Major**, with right and left hand:

Again, you can hold down the left hand note while playing the right hand chord
4 times:

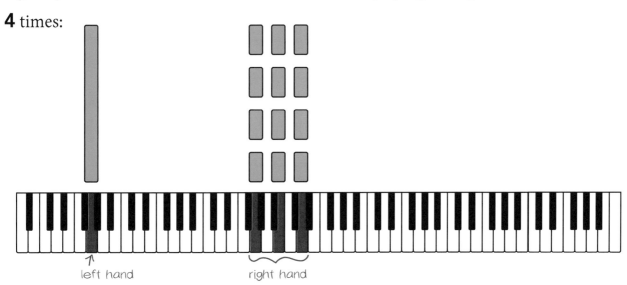

Or you can hold down the right hand chord while playing the left hand note
4 times:

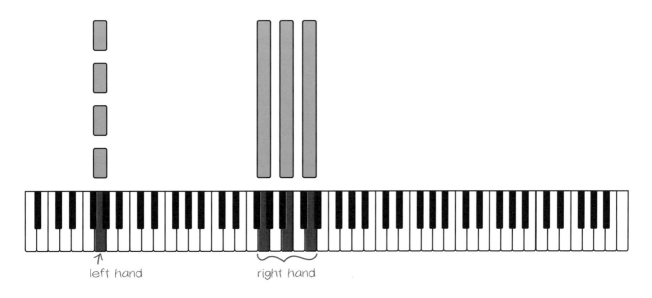

Or you can use a **Broken Chord** in the right hand in various ways:

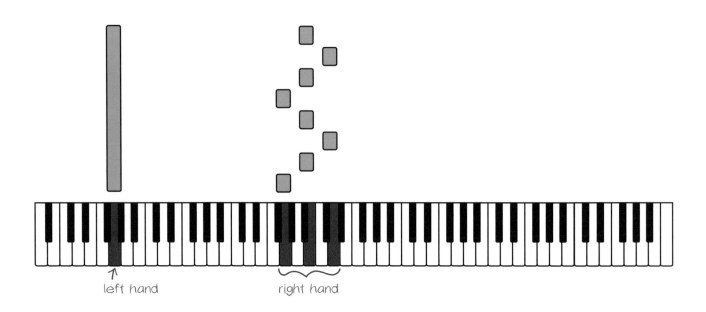

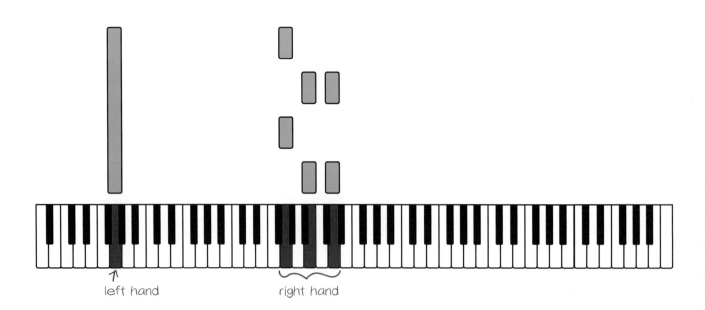

Use whichever pattern you like, or invent your own!

Here's the second chord, **D Major**:

left hand   right hand

Again, use whichever pattern you prefer from above.

Now, try playing **4 counts on G** and then **4 counts on D**. Go back and forth a few times.

When you're comfortable with **G** and **D**, here's **E Minor**:

left hand   right hand

And the last chord, **C Major**:

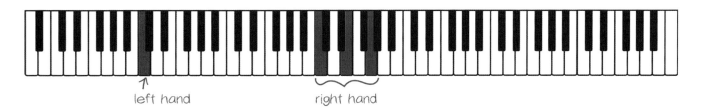

left hand   right hand

Now you can play the whole chord progression, with **4** counts each:

G   D   Em   C

Like many songs do, you can just repeat this chord progression on a **loop**:

G D Em C / G D Em C / G D Em C etc.

End on whichever chord you like. Ending on **G** will sound the most resolved, followed by **Em**, then **D**, and **C** will sound the least resolved.

If you want, you can try repeating the whole process on your own with the same infamous 4-chord progression in yet another key:

D   A   Bm   G

Here are the chord diagrams for these chords— for the rest you're on your own. (Or you can refer to pages 82-85 for help.)

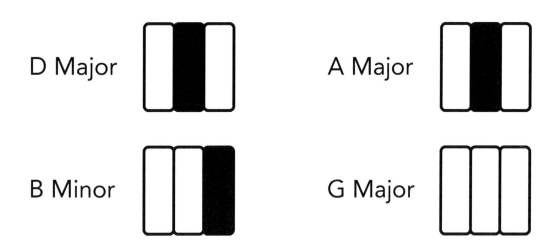

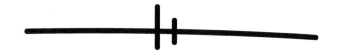

5. Some Chord Progressions to Try

Now, we're gonna give you some short chord progressions to try, all with chords that start on white notes (the only ones we've learned so far).

How to read the following pages:

Each chord progression takes up just one line, and to play it, just **loop** the same line over and over.

For example, here is a list of chord progressions:

Am F Dm E
Em C Am B
Bm G Em C

This shows 3 separate short chord progressions, meant to be played **one at a time** in a **loop**. For example, take just the first line, and play 4 beats on each chord in this order:

Am F Dm E / Am F Dm E / Am F Dm E etc.

Play the loop as long as you want, and decide for yourself which chord to end on. Some ending chords will sound better than others— use your ear to decide which one you like.

Then, move on to try an entirely different song using one of the other progressions:

Em C Am B / Em C Am B / Em C Am B etc.

List of Chord Progressions

Feel free to refer back to our list of chord diagrams on page 42 to help you remember how to play each chord below. After some practice, you'll start to memorize the chord shapes, so you can refer to the diagrams less and less.

Here's a super happy chord progression in several keys:

C F G F

E A B A

A D E D

Here's a super sad chord progression in several keys:

Dm Gm Am Gm

Em Am Bm Am

Gm Cm Dm Cm

Here's a sweet one in several keys:

C Dm Em Dm

G Am Bm Am

F Gm Am Gm

Here's a darkly epic one in several keys:

Am G F G

Em D C D

Bm A G A

(Remember, to play a chord progression, pick one line at a time and play it on a **loop**, like **C F G F** / **C F G F** / **C F G F** etc.)

6. Chords That Start On Black Notes

Now let's learn all the Major and Minor chords that start on black keys.

First of all, let's clarify the naming of these chords, since this can be a little confusing. Many people get **Sharp** & **Flat** mixed up with **Major** & **Minor**. For chords that start on black notes, we'll be using both at the same time, so let's just review to make sure we keep it straight:

E is a white **note**.

E♭ ("E Flat") is a black **note**.

Em ("E Minor") is a minor **chord** that starts on **E,** a **white note.**

E♭m ("E Flat Minor") is a minor **chord** that starts on **E♭,** a **black note.**

And the extra confusing part:

E♭ means **E Flat <u>Major</u>**. This is a **major** chord that starts on **E♭,** a **black note.** Many people get tripped up on a chord like this and play **E Minor** instead of **E Flat Major**.

Chords that start on black notes are also are a little trickier with finger placement.

Let's take **E♭ Major**, for example. Here's the chord diagram:

E♭ Major

The root note of **E♭ Major** is **E♭** *(not E!)*. So put your thumb here:

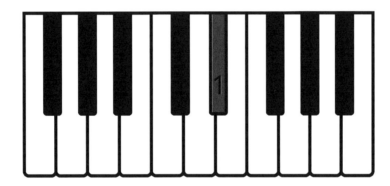

Now, finger 3 goes on a white note about the same distance to the right as before—but this time, since your thumb is on a black note, you'll want to place your middle finger on the *skinny part* of the white note to be comfortable:

play skinny part

Then, let finger 5 find its black note:

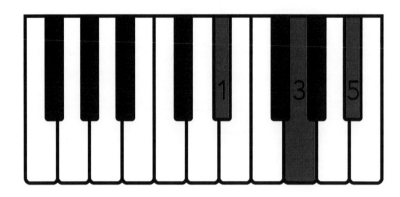

There you have it, E♭ **Major**.

Let's do another example— B♭ **Major**. Here's the chord diagram:

B♭ Major

Here's the root note:

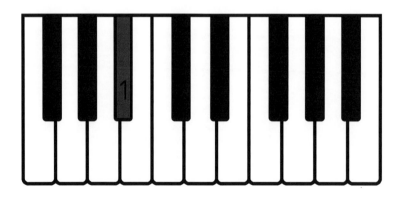

Then let your middle finger settle on this white note on the skinny part:

Then let your pinky settle on this white note, also on the skinny part:

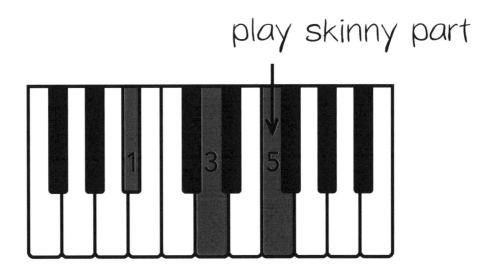

Voilà, **B♭ Major**.

There are also some chords where Major and Minor have the exact same colors—
D♭ Major & **D♭ Minor** are both *black-white-black*, and **A♭ Major** & **A♭ Minor** are also both *black-white-black*.

For **D♭ Major** and **D♭ Minor**, look how you play the *higher* white note for Major and the *lower* white note for Minor:

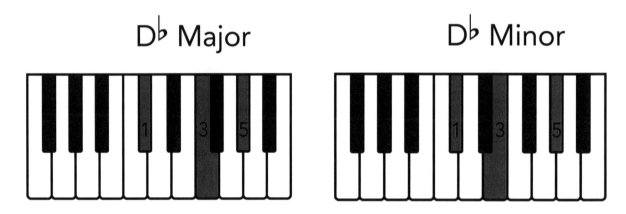

Since a showing a white note in the middle of the chord diagram doesn't help you figure out *which* white note, we write the chord diagrams like this:

Same issue with **A♭ Major** and **A♭ Minor**:

A♭ Major   A♭ Minor

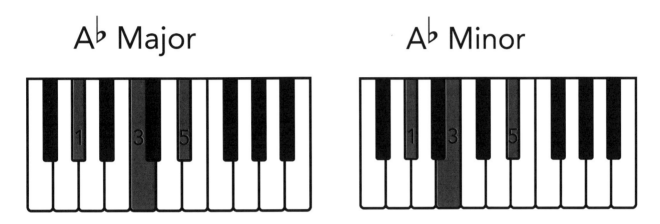

So here are the chord diagrams:

A♭ Major   A♭ Minor

So, now that we've covered our bases, here are **all the Major and Minor Chords that start on black notes:**

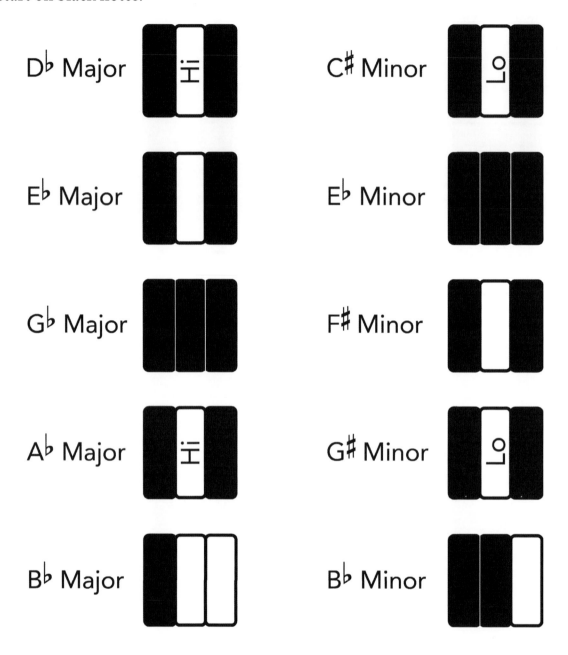

You may notice that three of the minor chords use the *sharp* name instead of the equivalent *flat* name. Technically, you can use either the *sharp* or the *flat* name for all of them. But in practice, the names are much more common as listed here (for music theory reasons beyond this book). **If you get stuck, refer to pages 82-85.**

Congrats, you've officially learned <u>every</u> major and minor chord in the Universe!

Here are a few more chord progressions you can try with your newfound freedom (remember, just play one line at a time on a **loop**):

Cm A♭ Fm G

Fm B♭m Cm B♭m

G♭ E♭m B B

B♭ Dm E♭ E♭m

67

7. How to Deal with Other (non-Major/Minor) Chords

There's one more thing you need to know before you look up chords to your favorite songs on your own.

So far, we've covered only Major and Minor chords, but there are lots of other types of chords you may come across. Luckily, you can just replace most of these complicated-sounding chords with simple Major or Minor chords, and they'll still fit with the song. In later books in this series, we'll learn how to play many of these chords, but for now you can use the following substitutes:

Any of these chords you can **replace with a Major chord**:

6 chords (**C6**, **G6**, **D♭6**, etc.),

Major 7 chords (**Cmaj7**, **Gmaj7**, **D♭maj7**, etc.),

7 chords (**C7**, **G7**, **D♭7**, etc.),

Major 9 chords (**Cmaj9**, **Gmaj9**, **D♭maj9**, etc.)

9 chords (**C9**, **G9**, **D♭9**, etc.),

add 9 chords (**Cadd9**, **Gadd9**, **D♭add9**, etc.),

11 chords (**C11**, **G11**, **D♭11**, etc.), and

Major 13 chords (**Cmaj13**, **Gmaj13**, **D♭maj13**, etc.)

13 chords (**C13**, **G13**, **D♭13**, etc.)

… can all be replaced with simple major chords: **C**, **G**, **D♭**, etc.

Any of these chords you can **replace with a Minor chord**:

Minor 6 chords (**Cm6**, **Gm6**, **D♭m6**, etc.),

Minor 7 chords (**Cm7**, **Gm7**, **D♭m7** etc.),

Minor Major 7 chords (**Cm maj7**, **Gm maj7**, **D♭m maj7**, etc.),

Minor 9 chords (**Cm9**, **Gm9**, **D♭m9**, etc.),

Minor add 9 chords (**Cmadd9**, **Gmadd9**, **D♭madd9**, etc.)

Minor 11 chords (**Cm11**, **Gm11**, **D♭m11**, etc.), and

Minor 13 chords (**Cm13**, **Gm13**, **D♭m13**, etc.),

… can all be replaced with simple minor chords: **Cm**, **Gm**, **D♭m**, etc.

Lastly, these chords **cannot be replaced with Majors or Minors**, so if you see one, just skip it for now:

Diminished chords (**Cdim**, **Gdim**, **D♭dim**, or **C°**, **G°**, **D♭°**, etc.),

Minor 7 ♭5 chords (**Cm7♭5**, **Gm7♭5**, **D♭m7♭5**, etc.),

Augmented* chords (**Caug**, **Gaug**, **D♭aug**, or **C+**, **G+**, **D♭+**, etc.), and

Suspended** chords (**Csus**, **Gsus**, **D♭sus**, etc.).

> *Sometimes you can replace **Augmented** chords with their **Major** equivalent (**C**, **G**, **D♭**, etc., but sometimes this will clash with the song.)

> **Sometimes you can replace **Suspended** chords with either their **Major** or **Minor** equivalent (**C** or **Cm**, **G** or **Gm**, **D♭** or **D♭m**, etc., but sometimes this will clash with the song.)

8. Slash Chords

Slash Chords are chords that are written like **G/B** or **Am/C** or **Fm/B♭**. We call them **Slash Chords** because they literally have a *slash* (/) in them. (This is very sophisticated stuff.)

When you see a slash chord, don't worry— you don't have to play two chords at the same time. There's actually only one **chord**: the part *before* the slash. The part *after* the slash is a **single note** for your **left hand** to play.

For example, let's try **G/B**:

G is the *chord* (**G Major**), and **B** is the *note* you play in your left hand, like this:

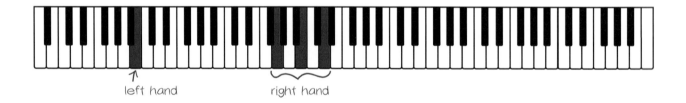

left hand   right hand

You'll recall that normally your left hand plays the **root note** of the chord. So we use **slash chords** to indicate when your left hand should play a note other than the root. This changes the sound of the chord substantially.

Here's another example— **Fm/B♭**:

Fm is the *chord* (**F Minor**), and **B♭** is the *note* you play in your left hand, like this:

left hand   right hand

Here are some chord progressions to try out some of the cool sounds that can be achieved with the creative use of slash chords:

A♭ E♭/G Fm D♭
Fm Fm/A♭ C/G C/E
G♯m/E G♯m/C♯ A A/B
B♭ E♭/B♭ Fm/B♭ E♭/B♭
C C/B♭ F/A Fm/A♭ C/G D/F♯ F B♭/E♭

Note that when playing with a group (like a band), the single note *after* the slash is often played only by the bass player, while other instruments play only the chord in a higher octave. But when playing solo piano, you usually want to play the bass player's part with your left hand.

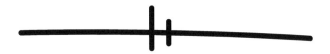

9. Learning Songs Out in the Wild

There is (always) more to learn, but at this point you're ready to go out in the wild (i.e, on the internet or in random music books) and start playing some songs of your choosing using their chord progressions.

Instead of choosing songs for you and putting them in this book, we instead encourage you to look some up on your own, because that way you can focus on songs you're excited to learn.

There's one last thing before you venture into the chaotic world of chord progressions on the internet: let's walk through the process of finding and interpreting chords so you're fully prepared.

Let's say you want to learn "The House of the Rising Sun," a traditional folk song popularized by the Animals.

Activate your internet device, and search for:

```
The House of the Rising Sun Chords
```

Something in the first few results is usually a good one. No, don't click on that ad!

Here's a result from *UltimateGuitar.com*, usually a reliable source for chord progressions (as of 2022):

```
        Am   C        D           F
There is a house in New Orleans
        Am        C      E
They call the "Rising Sun"
          Am        C       D         F
And it's been the ruin of many a poor boy
     Am     E          | Am | C | D | F | Am | E | Am | E |
And God, I know, I'm one
```

Then, all you have to do is play the chords written above the words. In this song, each chord is played for **6** counts.

(There's no surefire way to tell how many counts to play for each chord when you're looking them up online— the best way is just to sound it out, or *listen to the song* and see if you can figure it out. If you find this frustrating after repeated attempts, you may prefer learning to **Read Music** or **Play By Ear**.)

Chord symbols are usually written right above the word you sing when the chord starts (although the accuracy of this placement varies on the internet).

```
    Am  C      D         F
There is a house in New Orleans

    Am       C    E    E
They call "The Rising Sun"

    Am       C    D       F
And it's been the ruin of many a poor boy

    Am   E       Am C D F Am E Am E
And God, I know I'm one
```

In other words, the chord progression is:

Am C D F
Am C E E
Am C D F
Am E
Am C D F
Am E Am E

Try singing along while playing if you wish— you can play each chord just once while you're singing, or you can try to sing *while* playing **6** counts on each (not an easy feat).

Or just play the chords and see if you can hear in your head how the song fits with the chords.

Let's try one other example— "Happy Birthday."

Search the internet for:

Happy Birthday Chords

Here we are, again from *UltimateGuitar.com*:

```
              A            E
Happy Birthday to you
              E            A
Happy Birthday to you
              A7                   D
Happy Birthday dear (name)
              A        E    A
Happy Birthday to you
```

As we learned, we can replace **A7** with **A Major** (written as **A**), and it will still fit perfectly with the song.

Now, just play the chords written above the words.

In this song, all chords get **3** counts except for the very last line, where we've notated how many for each chord.

(Again, to figure out how long to play each chord on your own, the quickest way is to *listen to the song* and see what sounds right. Later in this series, we'll get into playing rhythm more precisely, but don't let that stop you from diving in and sounding it out as well as you can.)

```
       A         E
Happy Birthday to you


        E         A
Happy Birthday to you


        A         D
Happy Birthday dear (name)


      A(2)    E(1)  A(1)
Happy Birthday  to    you
```

Playing Chords from Sheet Music

Another way to learn the chords for a song is from **sheet music**. But instead of actually *reading* the music, just follow the chords.

Not all sheet music has the chords included— but a lot of it does. If you have any sheet music lying around, especially contemporary (non-classical) songbooks, there's a good chance some of it has the chords written out above the lines of music. Even sheet music for other instruments (violin, flute, trumpet, guitar, etc.) often has the chords included. A lot of people think the chords are intended only for guitar players, but they're actually intended for any instrument, including piano.

Here's how to tell:

This sheet music has the chords written above the notation. You can just ignore the notation (all the lines and black dots) and read only the chords above:

This sheet music has the chords plus the guitar shapes for those chords. (Just ignore the guitar shapes and play the chords as written.)

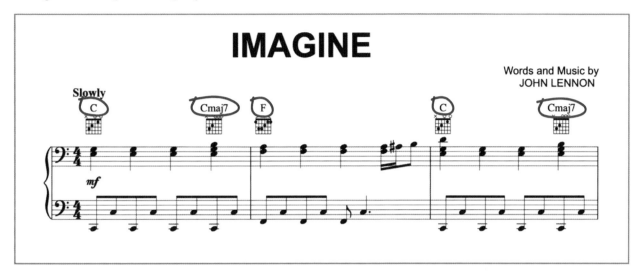

This sheet music does not have the chords written above, so you're out of luck. (Unless you decide to pursue learning to **Read Music**.)

If you don't have any sheet music lying around, there's always the internet.

Congratulations!

You've finished **Level 1** of How to Play the Piano with the **Chords Method.** You can officially play a simplified version of almost any song in the world using your chord knowledge and the internet. Go forth and find the chords for a song you've always wanted to learn!

When you're ready to take your chord playing to the next level, continue with the next book, **Level 2** of the **Chords Method f**or piano. There we'll learn lots of new and colorful tricks to add to your chord-playing, including: suspended chords, augmented chords, diminished chords, chord inversions, spread triads, open voicings, and more.

If you want to try out a different way of approaching music, try a different musical pathway: learning to **Play By Ear**, **Read Music**, **Improvise**, or the **Write Songs**. Or you can make a sideways move and try a different instrument like **Guitar**. (Fingerprint has a range of materials planned for all of the above.) There's no correct musical pathway— there's only YOUR musical fingerprint.

If you're unclear on anything you learned in this book, just go back to that part of the book and work through it repeatedly until it makes sense, or just do the whole book again. Repetition is key— with enough practice, patience, & persistence, music will become like a second language.

Appendix: All Major & Minor Chords

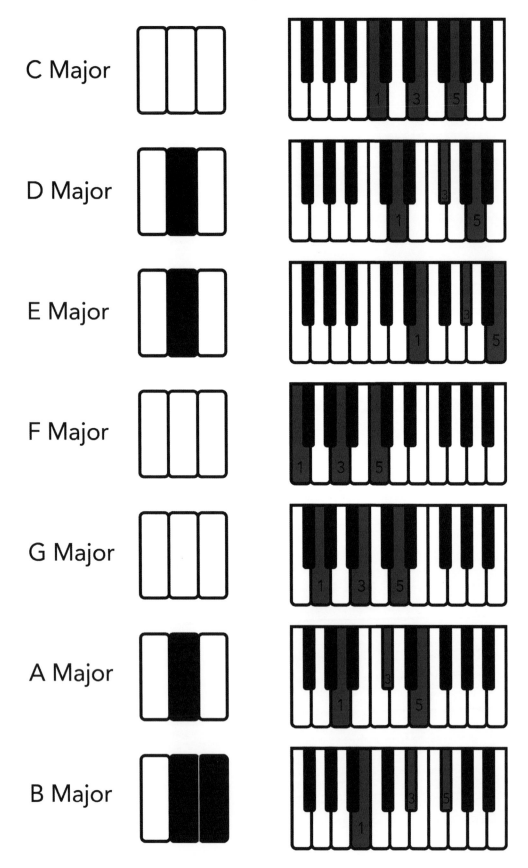

C Major

D Major

E Major

F Major

G Major

A Major

B Major

D♭ Major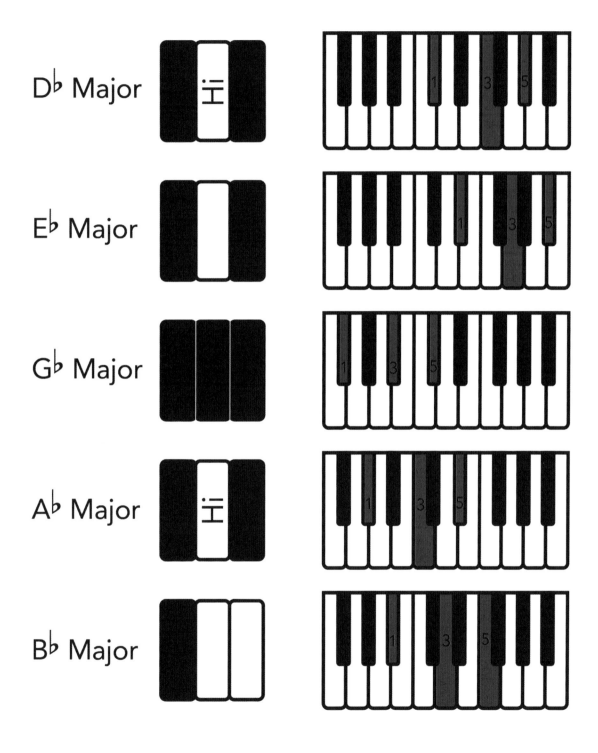

E♭ Major

G♭ Major

A♭ Major

B♭ Major

C Minor

D Minor

E Minor

F Minor

G Minor

A Minor

B Minor

C# Minor

E♭ Minor

F# Minor

G# Minor

B♭ Minor

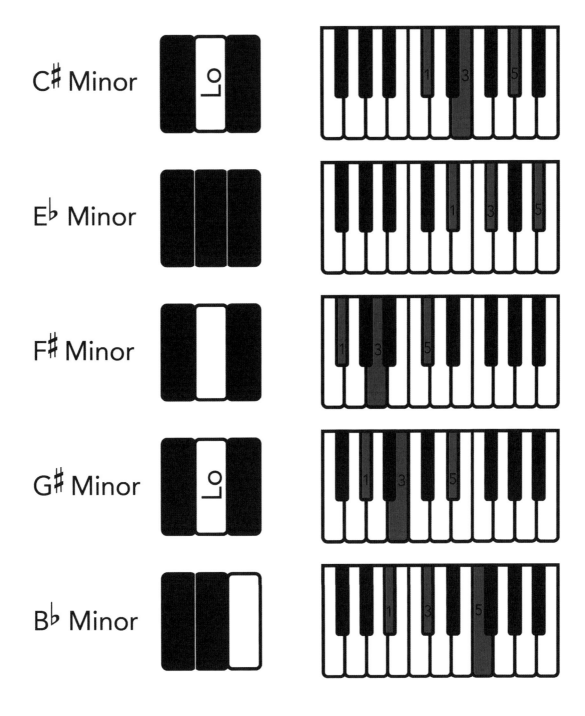

85

fingerprintmethod.com

Printed in Great Britain
by Amazon